SEO Basics

Tips For Small Business Owners

From the Library of the
New Thrive Learning Institute

Get Related Materials

from Our Free Library

Instant Access – Join Here

Click or type into your browser:

http://livesensical.com/go/byob/

Table of Contents

Introduction

Whether you've created a website already or are planning to create one in the near future, you know that's only half the battle. The other half is getting your website found in the search engines in hopes of attracting those interested in the type of products or services you offer.

Although there are a variety of ways to get your website found, this report focuses on Search Engine Optimization (SEO). Through effective SEO tactics, you can improve your search engine rankings for important terms, gain more traffic and do more business.

As I'm routinely asked to give SEO advice/tips, I decided to put my thoughts to paper. The resulting articles have been compiled to create this report. Because of this, you may see some "overlap" in the information presented.

Before I dive into the SEO tips, I'll give you my definition of both SEO and SEM. I'll also cover some of the most common SEO terms and give you explanations in plain English. This knowledge will help set the stage for everything that follows.

What Is Search Engine Optimization?

Search Engine Optimization

Search engine optimization, aka SEO, is the term that refers to the things you can do to improve your website's visibility in the search engines. Search engine optimization techniques focus on increasing the organic, or natural, traffic that you receive based on your ranking within the search engines.

The goal of search engine optimization is to ensure your website appeals to search engine crawlers, or bots. The search engines will take note of your site and its content, categorizing it in a way that will allow it to show up in the SERPs (search engine results pages) when certain keywords are typed.

Search engine optimization is achieved through a wide variety of methods. Many webmasters or SEO professionals will focus on proper keyword research, clarity in the setup of your website's headers, tags, file names and descriptions, external backlinking, internal cross linking, and quality content creation.

While each search engine uses its own algorithm for determining the ranking of every page that is indexed, it is possible to increase your rankings by making your site informative and visible via both on-page and off-page techniques. Sites that are designed with ease-of-use and quality information in mind tend to do better than those built sloppily and without a solid plan.

Search Engine Marketing

Search engine marketing, or SEM, is similar to search engine optimization but focuses less on natural rankings and more on the actual promotion of a website. SEM techniques generally include natural SEO but almost always branches out to include contextual or paid search advertising.

Paid search advertising models became more prominent in the late 1990's, after the search engines themselves became more popular. SEM focuses more on business-oriented websites and their overall online marketing strategies. Because many of the paid advertisements appear at the top of the search engines, the FTC in 2002 responded to complaints by clarifying that paid advertisements and website listings must be clearly denoted so that consumers do not confuse them with websites that have obtained high rankings naturally.

It really doesn't matter what type of website you have, whether it's personal or geared towards your business. Incorporating search engine optimization techniques into the creation and ongoing upkeep of your site will ensure you receive higher levels of traffic and, ultimately, greater success.

SEO Terminology - 5 Terms You Should Know

One of the reasons Search Engine Optimization seems so complex is that it there are so many foreign terms used. In this short article, I'll list some of the most common terms and will try my best to give you "geek free" definitions.

1. SEO

SEO stands for "Search Engine Optimization." This is a set of techniques and processes used by a SEO Specialist to improve your website's rankings in the search engines for a particular set of keywords, or keyword phrases.

Of course, the real goal is to increase targeted website traffic in hopes of generating new business. It's just that this is achieved through better search engine rankings. Studies have proven that the top 1-4 listings get far more traffic than the others found on the page.

2. SEM

SEM stands for "Search Engine Marketing." Defining SEM is a bit tricky as many authorities have varying ideas as to what the term means.

However, as a general rule, SEM Specialists use three distinct practices to promote their clients' websites:

- Traditional SEO techniques including both on-page and off-page search engine optimization strategies.

- Buying paid ads from the search engines that offer this type of service... primarily Google, Yahoo and Bing.

- Buying paid "inclusions" from the search engines. This is paying a search engine company for a guarantee that the website will be included in the search.

3. SERPs

SERPs stands for "Search Engine Results Pages." Basically, it's the page that is returned to you whenever you use a search engine.

The goal of SEO is to improve your web page's ranking amongst the other "organic" listings in the SERPs.

4. Keyword Phrase

A keyword phrase is any set of words that is searched upon by internet "surfers." It is the goal of the SEO Consultant to determine which keyword phrases are most relevant to your website/business and are likely to bring you targeted website traffic.

These keyword phrases are then used in the optimization process with the intent of getting your web page's strong rankings for the chosen terms (aka keyword phrases).

5. Backlinks

Defining backlinks is a challenge only because there are a variety of other terms that mean basically the same thing. You may also hear them referred to as text links, anchor text links, hypertext links, one-way links or contextual links.

A backlink occurs whenever another site links to yours. The link could come from an image or banner type graphic or it could be a linked piece of text.

For SEO purposes, the text links are of primary importance with the goal being to get links that include the keyword phrases you are optimizing for.

While there are hundreds of other SEO terms to learn, these will give you a good framework to build upon. Whether you are learning more so you can improve your own site or just want to be able to communicate better with your SEO Specialist, I encourage you to keep studying.

Don't Most Web Designers Know SEO?

The world of web design is complex and fraught with misinformation. Chief among them is the belief that most web designers have a solid understanding of Search Engine Optimization (aka SEO).

In truth, the exact opposite is true. Most web designers know very little about SEO and this includes those with college degrees in Website Design.

A friend of mine received a Bachelor's Degree in Web Design from a reputable University. When I asked her what she was taught concerning SEO she replied... "Not much."

They gave her their definition and spent a little time explaining the basic concepts. However, they weren't actually trained in the art and science we call SEO. They were told that work should be performed by an individual/company that specialized in Search Engine Optimization.

I agree with this as web designers are "artsy" by nature and not best suited to things that are highly technical. That's not to say that there aren't some who are good at both, just that it's probably the exception rather than the rule.

The real problem is that most clients know little about the web design process and mistakenly believe that their web designer has optimized their site for the search engines. As many web designers forget to discuss the topic with their clients, the site is put live without being optimized.

To improve your chances of getting a beautiful website that is well-optimized for the search engines, it's important you understand these three factors:

Web Design

In this phase, your web designer will work with you to create a nice looking website according to your project specifications. This part is primarily graphic in nature but it does form the foundation of the entire project.

Website Coding

After the website graphics are finished, the design will be coded such that it can be understood and displayed by browsers like Firefox, Internet Explorer, etc. Some web designers will use a program like Adobe's Dreamweaver to code the design while others will hire a web coder to do the process manually.

As a general rule, designs that are "hand coded" by a code specialist are more likely to follow the standards set by the Worldwide Web Consortium (aka W3C). They are also more likely to be "lighter" in their design, which is beneficial to SEO.

Search Engine Optimization

After the site has been designed and coded, the work can begin to optimize the website for the search engines. This is best performed by a SEO Specialist.

The SEO Specialist's job is to work closely with the client in an effort to understand their business and what outcome(s) they are looking to produce. With this information, the will begin the process of keyword selection and set about optimizing each page of the site.

In addition to the work performed to the site itself, the SEO Specialist will perform a variety of "off page" tasks. These tasks may include linkbuilding, social bookmarking, the creation of citations as well as many others.

As you can see, successful web design is a rather complex topic and frequently requires the work of several specialists. Armed with this information, you'll know what questions to ask to ensure your project is completed to your satisfaction.

After all, a beautiful website that receives little visitors won't help you achieve much in the way of new business.

Keyword Selection For Search Engine Optimization

Search Engine Optimization really isn't rocket science but there is a lot to know and consider when optimizing one's website.

At the forefront is the understanding of keywords/keyword phrases and what affect they have on your ability to get targeted website traffic.

What is a keyword/keyword phrase anyway?

It's the word, or words, that internet users are typing in when they conduct an internet search. Fortunately for us, there are a variety of tools that keep track of this incredibly valuable data.

With that understood, here are some tips to help you choose the right keywords for your website... keywords that will draw the specific type of visitors you are looking for.

Keyword tools

There are a variety of keyword tools, both free and paid. Unless you are an SEO professional, you'll probably want to use the free tool provided by Google.

To find it, simply conduct a search on Google for the term (aka keyword phrase), "Google Keyword Tool." As Google has done its job to optimize for this keyword phrase, you'll find it to be the first "organic" listing on page one of the results.

Search Volume

Search volume is an indicator that tells you how many times a particular keyword phrase is searched upon. The data is "search engine specific" so you will find that the numbers differ depending on which search engine's data you are looking at.

It's important to note that Google now tracks "local" and "global" search volume separately and can even tell you how frequently someone is searching the term with a mobile device.

Most SEO Consultants disagree as to the accuracy of the data so you should consider the data to be more "comparative" than accurate. For example, if "keyword phrase #1" is said to get 3,000 searches per month and "keyword phrase #2" is said to get 500, it's safe to say that keyword phrase #1 is more searched upon.

Competition

It's vital to remember that most search engines only show ten "organic" listings on any page of the SERPs (Search Engine Results Pages). Because of this, you are competing with the websites/web pages that are already ranked for the keyword phrase(s) you have chosen.

In order to get your web page listed on "page one" for a particular keyword phrase, you are going to have to outperform one of your competitors.

There are many factors to consider when gauging competition but the main ones include:

- On-page Optimization - In other words, how well have they optimized their page around the keyword phrase(s) they are ranking for.

- Age of the domain - Generally speaking, the older the domain, the better.

- Domain extension - Although you can improve the SEO of any website, those with a .com, .org, .net, .edu, .gov or a country specific domain tend to rank better than those with other extensions.

- Inbound links - The amount of links the page has from other websites as well as those coming from other pages of the site itself.

Intent

Before finalizing your keyword list, it's best to see if you can get into the mind of the person conducting the search. While your keyword research will tell you what keyword phrases are being searched upon, do you really know what they are looking for?

Here's a real-world example:

Let's say I wrote a book on emergency first aid and CPR and am looking for keyword phrases to promote my book. During my keyword research I find that the keyword phrase, "how to save a life," is searched more than 40,000 times per month. I get excited because this phrase seems perfect for promoting my new book. But is it?

I dig a little deeper and find that this phrase will be meaningless for me. Why? It's because the average searcher isn't looking to actually save a life, they're looking for information (lyrics, the music itself) for the song, "How To Save A Life" by The Fray!

The search volume is great, but the intentionality of the search is different than what it appears on the surface.

Keyword research is paramount to Search Engine Optimization and the ability to increase targeted website traffic. It's best to avoid rushing in as this is the foundation for which all other SEO tactics will be built upon.

Website Factors That Affect SEO

Search Engine Optimization is generally comprised of two distinctly different activities... optimizing the website itself , referred to as "on page" optimization, and increasing the authority of the website in the eyes of the search engines, referred to as "off page" optimization.

While both strategies must be employed for best effect, most SEO Consultants begin with the on page optimization work before beginning their off page optimization efforts.

In this article, I'll cover some of the things that can be performed to your website in order to increase its ability to achieve better rankings. First, however, you must understand that each and every page of your website needs to be SEO'd. This will not pose too much difficulty if your website is rather small but if you have dozens (or hundreds) of pages, the work to be done will be substantial.

Here are eleven website factors that may affect your SEO:

Meta Title

Your "meta title" information is added to the page source (i.e. your website coding). This may be done manually by your web designer or added through a WYSIWYG editor if your site uses some form of Content Management System (aka CMS). On some dynamic platforms, the meta title is created automatically as soon as the page is published.

Generally speaking, your meta title should be kept relatively short (no more than 60-80 characters) and should include the two-to-three keyword phrases you are specifically trying to optimize the page for.

Meta Page Description

Some may argue how much this affects SEO but there are other benefits to writing a good meta page description as well. Google will only display the first 156 characters (including spaces) of your page description so it's best to use that as your maximum length.

Your page description text should read well, include your primary keyword phrase at minimum and be somewhat exciting. The page description will generally be shown to searchers just beneath the clickable title. If your description tells of a benefit or evokes curiosity in the reader, you will enhance your ability to get visitors.

Meta Keywords

Most will tell you that meta keywords are worthless when it comes to SEO and I would tend to agree. However, if you are going to add meta keyword information I would recommend that you keep the amount to no more than about five terms in total.

It's bad practice to add dozens of meta keywords to each page and you may actually get penalized for doing so.

On Page Content

Your on page content should be unique to your website if at all possible and should also include the keyword phrases you are targeting. You don't need to worry about the specific "keyword density" anymore as that is mostly a thing of the past but it does help to include the terms you are specifically targeting at least once.

Your Web Page URL

If your website architecture allows you to control the name of each page, it's best to see that it includes your primary keyword phrase.

If you were targeting the term, "search engine optimization," for example, you might cause the url to be: domain.com/search-engine-optimization or even domain.com/search-engine-optimization.html Both examples work quite well so use whatever version is easiest for you to achieve.

Your Web Design

You may be surprised to see "web design" included in this list but it can affect your SEO in a variety of ways:

(1) Your design should be attractive and professional so as to keep your visitors on your site as long as possible .

(2) Your coding should be as "clean" as possible and should validate with the "W3C validation tool" whenever possible.

(3) Your images and coding should be optimized so as to maximize the speed of your site. This is good for both SEO and human visitors... no one likes to needlessly wait.

On Page Link Text

As you can control your on page link text, you can increase your optimization for a term by using the term in the text link that points to your other page.

The gain is generally considered minimal so this should only be done sparingly and only when the keyword phrase is relatively short.

Links Pointing To Other Sites

This topic may surprise you but most SEO Consultants agree... the search engines' believe that no one website is the "be all, end all" authority on a topic and therefore expect a website to link to others on the same topic.

Of course, there is a downside to this practice... you may find that the visitor leaves and never comes back. An intelligent strategy is to link to informational only sites, like Wikipedia, that do not provide competitive products or services.

Visit Duration

Many search engines now track how long your visitors remain on your site. The longer the average is, the more apt the search engines are to believe your site is relevant to the keyword phrase that brought them to your web page in the first place.

Visit Depth

In addition to visit duration, they can also track how many pages of your site the visitor looked at before leaving and which specific page they exited from.

You can see this data for yourself when viewing your web stats and can use the data to help you improve your visitor's experience.

Page Load Speed

I touched on this when I spoke about web design but your page load speed is also affected by the speed of your web hosting. It may not be a major factor, but the search engines are paying attention to how long your pages take to load.

It makes sense, really. The search engines do their best to deliver the best possible visitor experience and if your pages take forever to load, it's easy to conclude that many are probably irritated as a direct result.

If you address the majority of the topics contained in this article, you'll be on your way to well-optimized pages. With a strong SEO framework, you'll find that your off page optimization efforts yield better, and quicker results.

The Importance Of Building Quality Backlinks

If you've studied SEO for any length of time, you know that there are things you must do to your webpages themselves, called "on page optimization," and things external to your website, called "off page optimization."

While there are a number of tactics that fall into the off page optimization category, the most important is the building of quality backlinks. A backlink occurs whenever an image, a piece of text, or your full website url is linked "back" to your site from some other.

The best links are those that are "one-way," meaning that a site links to you but you do not link back to them. It can be beneficial to "trade links" (called reciprocal linking) with another webmaster for the purpose of gaining website traffic but it's not a strategy that will improve your search engine rankings or SEO.

As each page of your website should be optimized for 1-3 keyword phrases, it's best to build "anchor text links" (aka text links, hypertext links, hyper links, contextual links) that include the keyword phrases you are targeting. The more links you build, the better your ranking will be for the terms contained in the links.

Here's a perfect example of this in real life:

If you search Google.com for the term, "click here," you will find a page that gives access to the free Adobe Reader (a page off of Adobe.com) ranked in the first position.

This is an interesting/valuable observation as their page is not optimized for this keyword phrase at all. You won't find it in their Page Title, their Meta Page Description, or anywhere on the actual page itself.

Then how is this page ranked in the top spot for this term?

It's happening for one reason, and one reason only... a huge amount of backlinks have been built by webmasters from around the world, that link to this page. Want to guess what keyword phrase they've used when creating their links? That's right... they're linking the term, "Click Here," to the specific page that is ranking in the first position!

As I write this, Yahoo reports that 2,927,761 links are pointing to this page.

This shouldn't be taken to mean that you should abandon your on page optimization efforts, but it does reveal the power of anchor text backlinks.

The more links you build to your pages that include your targeted keyword phrases, the more likely your pages are to rank well for the terms... it's just that simple.

SEO Tips For Small Business Owners

While there are a variety of ways to increase targeted website traffic, every business owner should consider optimizing their website for the search engines.

Instead of putting all of your eggs in one basket, it's best to drive website traffic through several sources. This way, you can cast a wider net, resulting in more traffic, and track the efficacy of each source.

Before you begin, you should understand the core concepts of Search Engine Optimization (and Search Engine Marketing). In order to increase your website traffic and attract qualified prospects, you need to understand three things:

1.   **Everything related to SEO starts with an understanding of what a "keyword phrase" is.**

Anytime someone conducts a search on Google, or another search engine, they enter some text to start their search. In SEO terms, the entered text is called a "keyword" or "keyword phrase."

If you know what keyword phrases your prospects are entering when looking for the type of information, products or services you offer, you will know what phrases to optimize your web pages for.

2.   **Websites are not indexed or ranked by the search engines... each web page is indexed and ranked independent of any other.**

This is commonly misunderstood but so vital to understand! Just because you have one web page that ranks really well in the search engines, that doesn't mean that your others will also rank well.

Each page of your website must be uniquely optimized for a handful of keyword phrases... keyword phrases that are searched upon and those likely to attract your targeted audience.

If you pay close attention to the optimization of each page, you should see a dramatic improvement in terms of search engine placement.

3.   **Like it or not, you're competing against others!**

Some have a harder time with this concept than others but the truth remains the truth... in order to get your web page listed on page one of Google, you have to kick one of the currently listed web page's off!

This is valuable information because it will help you understand what you must do to achieve the ranking you're after.

Thorough analysis of the web pages currently listed for a particular keyword phrase will tell you how hard it will be to overtake one of them. You need to pay close attention to a number of elements including:

- How well is their page optimized for the keyword phrase?

- How old is their domain (the older the better)?

- How many links can be found that point to the page (the more the better)?

While there are other elements involved, these three are of primary concern. If you find you can outdo your competitor's web page in at least two of the three areas mentioned, you can probably kick them off the page and take their place.

After ensuring you are optimizing for a keyword phrase (or phrases) that are likely to bring you the kind of traffic you want, you'll often find it is the quantity of backlinks that make the real difference.

Of course, the quality of the backlinks is important too but if you are going to concentrate on one objective, it should be the building of links. Ensure your text links use the keyword phrases you are optimizing for and you'll find you quickly climb the ranks of the search engines.

Conclusion

As I mentioned in the Introduction, the articles that make up this report contain a number of "overlaps." This is important to note as the more times something was mentioned, the more crucial the information is.

I hope you found this information helpful and I hope it helps you improve your website's SEO.

Addendum

How to Avoid the Incredible Addiction to SEO in Online Marketing

You may have run into this addiction in promoting your own home business.

The statement runs around that "if you aren't on top of the search engine standings, you don't exist."

Unfortunately, that is <u>more false than true</u>.

This isn't to say that SEO isn't needed - it very much is - but **your business doesn't <u>have</u> to depend on using SEO for the entirety of its online marketing**.

That is just another form of addiction: giving complete control over one aspect of your business to a single source, such that your progress is measured only by a single metric. Much like an addict needing their next "fix", your marketing will go to all ends to maintain and expand your SEO results - even going to find places where you are ranking extremely well, but will never result in sales.

According to Forrester Research (as reviewed on <u>myHermes</u>), *30 percent of purchases start with an email from a retailer. 48 percent say that their buying process probably starts with reviews from a social platform like Facebook. The report said that <u>just 39 percent</u> of web* *transactions began from clicking on organic or paid search results.*

The key point is that search engine searches provide new prospects. Social platforms will provide relevance to their possible conversion to a buyer, as does any sales pages on your site - which is on-page content quality. Your relationships with customers will retain them as clients. 3/4's of this sequence doesn't require SEO.

Here's some other related links of interest down this line:

http://www.businessinsider.com/forget-apple-forget-facebook-heres-the-one-company-that-actually-terrifies-google-execs-2012-8

http://www.forbes.com/sites/halsinger/2012/09/18/who-competes-with-google-in-search-just-amazon-apple-and-facebook/

http://csi.mckinsey.com/Knowledge_by_region/Global/search

The summary is that while Google continues to dominate the mass of search engine queries, it's not going to give you anything but a <u>portion</u> of the customers you can have if you diversify your approach.

One key in all this is that the Internet looks to be simply amplifying <u>natural and traditional buying patterns</u> people have developed over the centuries. Yes, people respond to ads. Yes, people now utilize search to wade through the tons of data available.

But when YouTube is getting more search traffic than Google proper, and Amazon has a greater buying reach on mobile and the web, then you would be in error to solely and only work on making your site rank well on Google in order to get new customers.

Frankly, what this says is that you should take that site content and do several things:

1) Yes, get it optimized on-site so Google and the other search engines can categorize it easily. But also,

2) Convert it to several videos and put long keyword-rich descriptions and links on YouTube.

3) Convert it to an ebook and sell it via Lulu.com through Amazon (as well as through Smashwords, among others).

4) Compile your email list and maintain your relationships through it.

5) Create regular new content and cross-publish everything through the above.

There's a great short blog post about someone getting their book to the top ten list on Amazon via Lulu. (http://www.lulu.com/blog/2012/06/lulu-books-amazon-best-sellers/) You'll note that they promoted it to their list, which resulted in a flood of orders - catapulting their book onto the top-10 list where it stayed. And then it was easier to find (and buy) on Amazon. *So these elements tend start a "stacking effect" as they interact with the others.*

Which means you link to your Amazon author and book sales page from your site, and your ebook has hot-links to your site and your author page, and your emails have hot-links to a "resource" page which has these links, and so on.

This is the point here - that these all work <u>together</u>. Note that you can also give away that ebook you write to your list as an opt-in - or make a shorter version which is a come-on to buy the Amazon version (even give a discount coupon for those who do.)

The key point is that there is a much wider world out there than just SEO.

And if you do have a company who is doing your SEO, make sure they are also in syncopation with your overall Marketing planning.

SEO Basics - 31

You'll avoid addiction, as you understand how SEO is just a small (and getting smaller) part of your overall promotion-conversion-relationship marketing plan.

- - - -

Best of Luck to you!

Bonus

Get Related Materials

from Our Free Library

Instant Access – Join Here

Click or type into your browser:

http://livesensical.com/go/byob/